I Believe: Why Don't You?
The Bible is Not a Fairytale

I0172953

Copyright Page

For more information, please visit:

authoredwardfair.com[1]

Introduction: The Journey to Faith

Have you ever wondered if there is more to life than what we can see, touch, or measure? Have you felt the ache of questions that will not go away the longing to know if God is real, if faith has substance, if hope has a face?

If so, you are not alone.

I have walked that path, asked those questions, and wrestled with doubt. I have looked up at the stars and wondered, "Is there Someone out there?" I have faced challenges that made me question God's presence, and I have seen moments of grace that left me breathless.

This book is for people like you whether you are skeptical, searching, or simply curious. It is for those who have questions but are not sure where to turn for answers. It is for the believer who wants to strengthen their faith, and for the doubter who is open to the possibility that there might be something, or Someone, greater.

In the chapters ahead, we will explore the evidence historical, scientific, moral, and personal those points unmistakably to God. We will walk through the story of Jesus Christ, the ultimate proof of divine love. We will hear testimonies of lives transformed by faith, and we will wrestle with the reality of doubt.

But this is not just a book of arguments. It is an invitation.

An invitation to look again. To listen to the quiet voice within. To examine the evidence not just with your mind, but with your heart. To open the door, even a crack, and see if God steps in.

I do not have all the answers, but I have a story to tell a story of how God revealed Himself to me, through history, through Scripture, through creation, and through moments of quiet grace.

I believe. Why don't you?

As you read these pages, I invite you to consider: What if it is true? What if God is real, present, and longing to know you? What if faith is not blind, but the clearest vision of all?

Let us take this journey together.

Chapter 1: The Power of Creation

I have always been captivated by the natural world the rhythmic crash of ocean waves, the intricate patterns of a snowflake, the vast expanse of a starlit sky. Nature does not merely exist; it communicates. It whispers, "There's more here than meets the eye."

Creation itself is a testimony. When I walk along a shoreline and watch the waves shape the sand, or when I gaze at the stars on a crisp night, I am reminded that something or rather, someone put it all into motion.

Why don't you believe that?

Perhaps you've heard arguments suggesting the universe is a product of chance, a series of random events leading to the complexity we see today. But consider this: Could what appears as chance be purpose? Could the intricate design of our universe from the delicate balance of gravity to the complexity of a single cell be the fingerprint of a Creator?

The Apostle Paul wrote in Romans 1:20:

"For since the creation of the world God's invisible qualities his eternal power and divine nature have been clearly seen, being understood from what has been made, so that people are without excuse."

This verse emphasizes that God's attributes are evident in creation. The universe, in its vastness and intricacy, points to a Designer. The beauty, order, and complexity we observe are not mere coincidences but reflections of God's character.

Consider the fine-tuning of the universe. Scientists have discovered that the fundamental constants of nature are precisely calibrated to allow for the existence of life. Even slight variations in these constants would make the universe uninhabitable. This precision suggests intentionality, not randomness.

Look at a simple seed. Within it lies the blueprint for a towering oak, a brilliant flower, or a mighty tree that provides shade, fruit, and shelter. How does it know what to become? How does it unfurl from a tiny speck of potential into a living, breathing testament to life? This is not random. This is evidence of intention.

Psalm 19:1-2 declares:

"The heavens declare the glory of God; the skies proclaim the work of his hands. Day after day they pour forth speech; night after night they reveal knowledge."

The natural world is a canvas displaying God's glory. Every sunrise, every blooming flower, every chirping bird sings a song of praise to the Creator.

The complexity of life further underscores this point. The human body, for instance, is a marvel of engineering. Our eyes can distinguish millions of colors, our brains process vast amounts of information, and our hearts beat tirelessly throughout our lives. Such complexity and efficiency point to intelligent design.

Moreover, nature's beauty evokes a sense of awe and wonder. The majestic mountains, serene lakes, and vibrant sunsets stir emotions within us. This appreciation for beauty is not merely a human construct; it reflects the Creator's own nature. As the philosopher Augustine once said, "Who made these beautiful changeable things, if not one who is beautiful and unchangeable?"

Yet, despite this overwhelming evidence, some choose not to believe. They attribute the wonders of the universe to chance or dismiss them altogether. But as Romans 1:20 states, the evidence is so clear that people are without excuse.

So, why don't you believe?

Is it fear? Doubt? The overwhelming noise of a world that is taught you to dismiss the idea of a Creator. Or you have never taken a moment to look deeply beyond the surface of science and philosophy to listen to what creation is quietly saying: "I was made. You were made. There is a Maker."

In the chapters to come, we will explore the evidence of God's existence through history, science, personal stories, and scripture. But it all begins here with the natural world as a canvas of His glory.

Look up. Look around. Do you see what I see?

I believe. Why don't you?

Chapter 2: History Testifies

Archaeology and ancient texts confirm the truth of Scripture in ways too powerful to ignore. Repeatedly, discoveries made beneath the sands of time have affirmed what believers have long held to be true God's Word stands, no matter how many centuries pass.

Skeptics have long tried to dismiss the Bible as legend, but evidence keeps rising from the ground to challenge their doubts. When archaeologists uncovered the ruins of Jericho, they found collapsed walls just as described in the book of Joshua. The discovery of the Dead Sea Scrolls in 1947 revealed manuscripts dating back to 200 B.C. including the entire book of Isaiah almost word-for-word as we have it today. Such preservation across millennia is nothing short of divine.

I remember once hearing a young man challenge his pastor: "How do you know the Bible wasn't just made up?" The pastor smiled gently and said, "That is a fair question. But let me ask you this if it was made up, why does it keep proving itself every time someone tries to disprove it?"

Faith does not require archaeology to be real, but archaeology certainly strengthens faith. When we see with our own eyes that the places, names, and events of Scripture are grounded in historical fact, it moves belief from hope to conviction.

A Pastor's Healing in the Middle of Doubt

Years ago, in a small Midwest town, a pastor named Rev. Thomas was diagnosed with a serious autoimmune disease. The doctors were confident that even with treatment, his energy and memory would decline sharply. The church members rallied in prayer, but Rev. Thomas remained realistic his sermons shortened, and his memory did begin to fail.

One Sunday morning, he approached the pulpit to preach and found his notes were missing. Panic swept over him. He bowed his head silently and whispered, "Lord, if You want me to continue, you must speak through me." What followed stunned the congregation. Rev. Thomas preached for 45 minutes, not from notes, but with power and clarity he had not known in years. He quoted Scripture, shared stories from his childhood, and even recalled the names of everyone in attendance.

His healing was not immediate or total, but from that day forward, his mind was never as clouded again. Medical records showed no explanation for the improvement, but the church knew what had happened. The Bible calls us to walk by faith, not sight and Rev. Thomas walked on, carrying the truth of God's Word with each step.

In Financial Struggle

There was a young couple I once met during a revival meeting. They were newly married, expecting their first child, and struggling financially. The husband, Brian, had been laid off from a factory job. Rent was due, the car needed repairs, and they had less than $20 between them. They were devout believers, but the pressure of the situation pushed them to a crossroads.

They shared their burden with the revival speaker, who prayed with them and quoted Matthew 6:33: "Seek first the kingdom of God and His righteousness, and all these things will be added to you." That night, they gave their last five dollars in the offering not out of guilt, but in hope.

Two days later, Brian got a phone call for a job interview he had not even applied for. It was a supervisor who had seen his résumé from a year ago. Not only did Brian get the job, but they paid him back-pay for training time, and the position came with full benefits.

They never missed a rent payment again, and they credited it not to the five dollars but to the faith they put behind it. "God doesn't need your money," the wife once told me. "He just needs your trust."

A Child's Prayer

Children often remind us that faith does not need to be complicated. During a Vacation Bible School I attended in the 90s, one little girl named Sarah asked during prayer time if God could fix her dad's drinking problem. She was seven years old and did not understand theology, but she believed what we told her that God listens.

That Friday, her father showed up to the VBS closing ceremony sober. He had not been inside a church in years. He said something made him drive by the church on Monday and every day after. He never drank again. "I just didn't want to disappoint her," he said through tears, pointing at Sarah.

Faith the size of a mustard seed. That is all it took. A child asked, and God answered.

Biblical History is Still Relevant

Beyond personal testimony, there's biblical proof in history that resonates today. Take the apostle Paul's shipwreck on the way to Rome (Acts 27). For years, skeptics called it myth. But in the 1960s, divers off the coast of Malta discovered ancient Roman anchors right where Luke described. The seabed still bears the marks of that storm-tossed voyage.

We did not need that anchor to believe Paul's story but how amazing is it when God allows physical proof to surface centuries later?

A Living Word

I have come to understand the Bible is not just historically correct it is spiritually alive. It breathes into us when we read it, convicts us when we wander, and comforts us when we hurt. The Bible says, "The Word of God is living and active, sharper than any two-edged sword" (Hebrews 4:12). I have seen it cut through doubts. I have seen it pierce pain. I have seen it heal.

Faith does not mean blind belief. It means looking at what is real in history, in lives changed, in promises kept and choosing to trust what it points to.

Why don't you, believe?

Chapter 3: Science and Faith

For centuries, science and faith have often been seen as opposing forces as though belief in God must be abandoned in the face of scientific discovery. But is that really the case? Science and faith are not in conflict. Instead, they reveal various aspects of the same truth: a universe created and sustained by an intelligent, loving God.

Why don't you believe?

The Myths of Conflict

Some would argue that science, with its focus on observation and experimentation, has no room for faith. They claim that faith is blind, that it relies on superstition, and that it must be abandoned in favor of reason. But history tells a different story.

Men and women of faith laid the very foundations of modern science. Think of Isaac Newton, who discovered the laws of motion and gravity but also wrote extensively on theology. Or Johannes Kepler, who described the orbits of planets as "thinking God's thoughts after Him." These pioneers did not see a conflict between studying the natural world and believing in its Creator. In fact, they believed that the order and design of the universe were reflections of God's character.

The Bible itself encourages us to observe and learn from nature. Psalm 19:1-2 declares:

"The heavens declare the glory of God; the skies proclaim the work of His hands. Day after day they pour forth speech; night after night they reveal knowledge."

Fine-Tuning the Universe

Modern science has revealed just how finely tuned the universe is. Consider the fundamental constants of nature the strength of gravity, the charge of the electron, the speed of light. Even a slight change in these values would make life impossible.

Astrophysicist Paul Davies once remarked, "The impression of design is overwhelming." This is not mere coincidence; it is evidence of a universe designed with purpose.

Think of the complexity of the human cell. It is a microscopic world of machines, each working together with stunning precision. DNA carries the information needed to build and support life, like a complex instruction manual written in a four-letter alphabet. Could this intricate design really be the product of random chance? Or does it point to a Designer who knows us intimately even at the cellular level?

The Limits of Science

Science is a powerful tool for understanding the natural world, but it has limits. It can tell us how the universe works, but not why it exists. It can describe the chemical reactions in the brain, but not the nature of love, hope, or purpose.

Faith steps in to answer these deeper questions. Why is there something rather than nothing? Why do we long for justice, beauty, and truth? Why do we love, create, and hope? These are questions science alone cannot answer but faith in God can.

Testimony of God's Presence in Science

Let me share a story from my own life that illustrates how God's hand works even when we think we understand everything with human logic and science.

It was the winter of 1991, and I was working in the emergency department to complete paramedic training. That morning, around 5:30 a.m., I had a vision clear as day that I would roll my car on the drive home. The vision showed me the exact curve in the road where it would happen. At first, I thought it was just a dream or my imagination, but the feeling would not leave me.

I decided to stay an extra half hour, thinking I could change fate. When I finally left and drove home, it was snowing lightly. I slowed down as I approached the curve, dropping my speed from 35 mph to just 15 mph no car should roll at that speed, right?

But as I reached the curve, my car hit a patch of ice, spun, and rolled onto its roof. It was as though God was reminding me that no matter how much we try to control our circumstances, His plans are greater. Amazingly, I was not hurt. The car only had minor damage to the mirror and window, which I fixed for just $35.

Looking back, I see this event not as a punishment or coincidence, but as a reminder of God's sovereignty. Even in moments where science might explain the physics of a car rolling, God's presence was undeniable. He was there, guiding me, protecting me, and reminding me of His power.

Bridging the Gap

Many scientists today far from rejecting faith see science to appreciate God's creation. Francis Collins, a renowned geneticist and leader of the Human Genome Project, described his journey from atheism to faith in his book The Language of God. He writes:

"The God of the Bible is also the God of the genome. He can be worshiped in the cathedral or in the laboratory."

This resonates with me deeply. God is not confined to the walls of a church. His fingerprints are everywhere in the complexity of DNA, the laws of physics, the beauty of a sunset, and the gentle voice in our hearts that calls us to Him.

Faith and Reason Together

It is often said that faith and reason are opposites, but that is a false dichotomy. Faith is not blind belief; it is trust based on evidence. Reason helps us understand the world, and faith gives it meaning. Together, they form a complete picture.

Consider this: if the universe is so complex and finely tuned, doesn't it make sense that it has a purpose? If life is so intricate, doesn't it suggest a Giver of life? If love, justice, and beauty stir our hearts, doesn't that point to a Creator who embodies these virtues?

A Second Testimony: God's Plan in Life Changes

Another time, God's hand was clear in my life when I was serving as a paramedic and firefighter. After years of service, my wife and I debated whether to move from Pennsylvania to Florida. We faced financial challenges and uncertainty, but one day, I felt prompted to act.

I called my wife and asked her to look for a home in Florida. She found a trailer for $2,000. We bought it before the ad even appeared in the paper a sign of God's perfect timing. We moved quickly, secured work, and within days, I transitioned into a completely different field. God orchestrated the details, from housing to employment, in a way that only He could.

This was not just a stroke of luck it was God's plan, unfolding in real time. It was a reminder that faith means stepping forward, even when we cannot see the full picture. God meets us there.

Conclusion: The Harmony of Science and Faith

Science explores the "how" of the universe, and faith explains the "why." Together, they tell a complete story of a world created with purpose, governed by laws, and sustained by a loving Creator.

I believe because I see God's hand in the natural world, in the discoveries of science, and in the stories of my life and the lives of others. The intricate design of the universe, the mysteries of life, and the undeniable presence of God in everyday moments compel me to trust in Him.

Why don't you believe?

Chapter 4: The Moral Compass

One of the most convincing and personal arguments for God's existence is not found in distant galaxies or complex theology. It is found within us. It is the quiet whisper that says, "This is wrong," when we lie, and the peace we feel when we choose kindness over cruelty. It is the part of us that long for justice, even when it does not help us directly. This is the moral compass etched into the heart of every human being. It does not point north. It points to God.

I believe because morality speaks of God. Why don't you?

The Inner Law That Knows No Borders

Every culture ancient or modern, religious, or secular has moral codes. Even those who have never read the Bible believe it is wrong to kill, lie, or steal. They honor self-sacrifice and condemn cruelty. Why is that?

Romans 2:14-15 offers a divine explanation:

> "When Gentiles, who do not have the law, do by nature things required by the law... they show that the requirements of the law are written on their hearts."

God has written His law not just on stone tablets, but in human hearts.

The Paramedic and the Drunk Driver

During my early years as a paramedic, I was called to a terrible accident. A young man had been driving under the influence and slammed into another vehicle. He walked away with scratches. The other driver a young mother lay unconscious, barely clinging to life.

As I worked to stabilize the scene, I could feel anger building in me. I was not supposed to judge, only help. But inside I raged how could he be so careless?

Later that night, I sat in my rig, processing the emotions. That is when a verse I had not read in months came to mind:

"Forgive, as the Lord forgave you" (Colossians 3:13).

I did not want to. But I knew I had to. That moment of choosing grace over rage did not just help me it changed me. It reminded me that morality is not about behavior. It is about heart transformation.

History Confirms the Moral Law

Thousands of years before Jesus walked the earth, civilizations recorded moral standards eerily like the Ten Commandments. The Code of Hammurabi, discovered in modern-day Iraq, dates to around 1750 B.C. It has laws against murder, theft, adultery, and lying under oath proof that God's moral fingerprint predates even Scripture's written form.

Even more fascinating are the Ebla Tablets, unearthed in Syria in the 1970s. These clay records, over 4,000 years old, mention biblical cities like Sodom and Gomorrah and have laws forbidding injustice and corruption aligning closely with the moral teachings of the Bible.

When people say morality is man-made, they often overlook that these ancient codes across continents say the same things. That is not coincidence. That is confirmation.

Without God, Morality Collapses

If there is no God, then what makes one set of morals better than another? If all morality is subjective, then who says kindness is better than cruelty? Why should we seek justice if there is no eternal right or wrong?

Philosophers have wrestled with this. Without a higher standard, morality becomes preference. But with God, we have a foundation. A righteous Judge. A divine Lawgiver. Someone who not only defines good and evil but embodies it.

A Child's Choice to Tell the Truth

Let me tell you about a seven-year-old boy named Marcus. I met him during a children's program at church. His mother told me he had been caught lying at school. That night, during story time, we talked about honesty and how God sees even what we hide.

The next morning, Marcus went to his teacher and confessed. No one told him to. He simply said, "God knew, and I don't want to lie anymore." That is not social conditioning. That is conscience. That is the still, small voice of the Spirit at work in a child.

When Science Meets the Soul

Even scientific studies cannot explain why humans feel moral obligation. Evolution may account for group survival, but it does not explain sacrificial love or why people risk their lives for strangers. It does not explain why a soldier jumps on a grenade, or why a nurse stays by a dying patient's side when they could go home safely.

That is not biology. That is something divine.

In Conclusion

Our moral compass is not a social invention. It is a signature from God a reminder that we were created in His image and wired to reflect His nature.

History testifies through ancient laws. Scripture testifies through its divine coherence. But it is our own conscience our unseen guide that gives the most personal witness of all.

I believe because my soul cries out for justice, mercy, and love. And the One who gave me that voice still speaks through it. Why don't you?

Chapter 5: Changed Lives, Changed Hearts

When we talk about proving God's existence, we often look at the vastness of the universe, the precision of nature, and the compelling logic of morality. But there is another kind of evidence that speaks just as powerfully the transformed lives of people who have met God's grace and truth.

I believe because I have seen and experienced the life-changing power of God. Why don't you?

The Power of Personal Testimonies

There is something undeniably compelling about a personal story. When someone shares how they were once lost, broken, or wandering, and then met God and found purpose, peace, and joy, it speaks louder than any argument or theory. These testimonies are not just anecdotes they are living proof that God is real, active, and involved in our lives.

In John 9, we read the story of a man born blind whom Jesus healed. The religious leaders questioned him repeatedly, trying to discredit Jesus. But the man simply replied, "One thing I do know. I was blind but now I see!" (John 9:25). His life was the testimony. He did not need a theological debate his experience spoke for itself.

A Personal Story of God's Intervention

I have shared glimpses of my own journey but let me tell you another story that shows how God's hand guided my life in a profound way.

It was early spring in 2021. I was living in Florida, comfortable with my routine, but something kept tugging at my heart. I could not shake the feeling that I needed to move back north to be near my aging father. My wife and daughter agreed, even though it meant leaving the warmth and comfort of our home.

I took a step of faith, listing our house for sale online late one Sunday night. By the next morning, I received a call from a man in Ohio who was in Florida looking for a home. He agreed to buy our house for cash $55,000 the very next day.

Now we faced another challenge: finding a home up north. My father and sister began searching, and within three days, they found a house in Niles, Ohio. It had everything we needed: a two-car garage, a basement, a first-floor master bedroom. The price? Exactly $55,000 the same amount we sold our Florida home for.

That was not coincidence. That was God orchestrating the details of our lives, providing exactly what we needed at exactly the right time. It was as though He was saying, "Trust Me. I have this."

God's Power to Transform Lives

It is not just my story. Countless others have experienced God is transforming power. I think of people like Jill Kelly, the wife of NFL quarterback Jim Kelly, who has openly shared how God's grace sustained her family through the heartbreak of losing a child to a rare disease. In the face of unimaginable grief, she found strength and hope in Christ, writing, "God is all in. He is fully committed to you. He will not forget. He will not give up. He is not stuck or confused. He has you fully, wholeheartedly, completely."

Or consider John Newton, the former slave trader who met God's mercy and became a preacher and the author of Amazing Grace. His life was a testament to the reality of God's power to change even the hardest hearts.

These stories, old and new, echo the same truth: God is real, and He is in the business of changing lives.

A Story of Healing

One of the most incredible stories I have seen happened in my own family. My wife, Debbie, was diagnosed with kidney failure and had been on dialysis for months. The doctors told us that recovery was unlikely.

Statistically, only a small percentage of dialysis patients regain kidney function after a certain point.

But in mid-April of 2021, Debbie's lab numbers began improving rapidly and unexpectedly. By early May, her doctors took her off dialysis completely. The timing was perfect. Just weeks later, her father suffered a massive stroke, and Debbie was able to travel to Florida with our daughter to care for him.

Looking back, I cannot help but see God's hand in this. It was not just a lucky break or a fluke of medicine. It was a divine intervention, a miraculous answer to prayer that allowed Debbie to be where she was needed most.

What Transformation Looks Like

When God changes a life, it is not just about external circumstances. It is about internal transformation. It is about a heart made new, a mind renewed, a life redirected. It is about hope replacing despair, peace overcoming anxiety, and love conquering bitterness.

The Bible tells us in 2 Corinthians 5:17:

"Therefore, if anyone is in Christ, the new creation has come: The old has gone, the new is here!"

I have seen this truth play out in my own life, in my family, and in the lives of friends and strangers alike. I have watched addicts find freedom, broken marriages find healing, lonely hearts find community, and the lost find their way home.

Why Testimonies Matter

Testimonies are powerful because they are personal. They are not abstract arguments or distant stories; they are real people, living real lives, touched by the real God. They remind us that faith is not what we believe it is about what we experience.

When you hear someone say, "I was blind but now I see," or "I was lost but now I'm found," you are hearing the heartbeat of the gospel. You are hearing the voice of God saying, "I am here. I am real. I am ready to change your life, too."

Why Don't You Believe?

If you have ever doubted God's existence, I challenge you to look at the evidence not just in the stars or scriptures, but in the lives of those around you. Talk to people of faith. Listen to their stories. Hear how God has brought them through storms, lifted them from despair, and filled them with peace and purpose.

You are waiting for a sign, a miracle, or a voice from heaven. But sometimes, the clearest sign is the transformed life sitting right beside you.

I believe because I have seen God change lives my own, my family's, and so many others. Why don't you?

A Closing Invitation

In the next chapter, we will explore how fulfilled prophecies reveal God's knowledge of the future yet another powerful testimony of His existence and involvement in our world. But before we turn the page, I invite you to reflect:

Has God been at work in your life, even if you did not recognize it at the time? Has He placed people, circumstances, or opportunities in your path to draw you closer to Him? Are you ready to open your heart and let Him transform you, too?

I believe. Why don't you?

Chapter 6: Prophecy and Fulfillment

Some people believe in chance. Others place their trust in logic or science. Still others rely on their own strength or knowledge. But as I have journeyed through life and faith, I have come to trust in something far more powerful: God's Word, proven true through prophecy.

I believe because fulfilled prophecy is a signpost pointing to God. Why don't you?

What Is Prophecy?

Prophecy is more than a prediction it is a revelation of God's will and knowledge. Prophets throughout the Bible spoke of future events, not based on guesswork, but by divine inspiration. Unlike vague fortune-telling or generalized forecasts, biblical prophecies are precise, often against the odds, and often fulfilled in extraordinary ways.

God Himself declared in Isaiah 46:9-10:

"I am God, and there is no other; I am God, and there is none like me. I make known the end from the beginning, from ancient times, what is still to come."

Prophecy is one way God reveals His sovereignty, reminding us that nothing surprises Him and that His plans will prevail.

Prophecies About Jesus

One of the clearest examples of prophecy's fulfillment lies in the life, death, and resurrection of Jesus Christ. The Old Testament has over 300 prophecies about the Messiah, written centuries before Jesus was born. These prophecies speak of His birth, ministry, suffering, and ultimate victory.

For example:

- Micah 5:2 predicted the Messiah's birthplace: "But you, Bethlehem Ephrathah, though you are small among the clans of Judah, out of you will come for me one who will be ruler over Israel." Jesus was born in Bethlehem, fulfilling this prophecy exactly.

- Isaiah 53 describes the suffering servant, pierced for our transgressions, bearing our iniquities a prophecy fulfilled in Jesus' crucifixion.
- Psalm 22 foreshadows crucifixion in vivid detail, centuries before it was a known method of execution: "They pierce my hands and my feet... They divide my clothes among them and cast lots for my garment."

These prophecies are so specific and detailed that their fulfillment cannot be dismissed as coincidence. They point to a divine Author who not only knows the future but orchestrates it for His purpose.

Prophecies in History

Prophecy does not stop with Jesus. The Bible has many prophecies about nations, cities, and historical events many of which have been fulfilled with remarkable precision.

Consider:

- Ezekiel 26 predicted the destruction of Tyre, describing how its debris would be thrown into the sea. Centuries later, Alexander the Great's forces dismantled the city's ruins and used them to build a causeway, fulfilling the prophecy exactly.
- Daniel 2 and Daniel 7 outlined the rise and fall of empires Babylon, Medo-Persia, Greece, and Rome long before they came to power.
- Zechariah 9:9 foretold the Messiah's entry into Jerusalem on a donkey, fulfilled by Jesus during His triumphal entry.

These are not vague guesses; they are detailed predictions that were fulfilled in ways only God could arrange. They remind us that history is not random it is directed by a sovereign hand.

A Testimony of Prophetic Fulfillment in My Life

I have seen prophecy not only in scripture but in my own life. Let me share a story that still amazes me.

Years ago, as I served as a paramedic and firefighter, I was deeply involved in my community but felt God calling me toward something more. I sensed that He had a greater plan, though I could not see the details. One day, after a particularly challenging shift, I remember praying, "God, if You have a purpose for me beyond this, show me."

A few weeks later, during a sermon at church, the pastor spoke directly about stepping out in faith, trusting God's plan, and listening to His call. He referenced Jeremiah 29:11:

"For I know the plans I have for you," declares the Lord, "plans to prosper you and not to harm you, plans to give you hope and a future."

I knew in my heart that God was speaking to me through that message. Shortly afterward, doors began to open for me to pursue ministry, writing, and teaching. Today, as I author this book and share these stories, I see that the prophetic promise of Jeremiah 29:11 was fulfilled in my life. God had a plan, and in His perfect timing, He revealed it.

Prophecy for Today and the Future

Prophecy is not about the past it points to the future, too. The Bible speaks of events yet to come: the return of Christ, the final judgment, and the establishment of God's eternal kingdom.

Revelation 21:4 gives us a glimpse of that future:

" 'He will wipe every tear from their eyes. There will be no more death or mourning or crying or pain, for the old order of things has passed away.'"

This is the ultimate fulfillment of God's plan a world made new, free from sin and sorrow. It is a promise we can hold onto, especially in times of uncertainty.

The Invitation of Prophecy

Prophecy is not just a puzzle to be solved; it is an invitation. It invites us to trust God, to see His hand in history, and to embrace His plan for our lives. It is a reminder that the same God who fulfilled promises in the past is faithful today and forever.

Why don't you believe?

When you read fulfilled prophecies in the Bible or hear testimonies of God's work in modern times, you are encountering a God who keeps His Word. His promises are trustworthy. His plans are good. And He invites you to be part of His story.

A Closing Reflection

In the next chapter, we will explore how the inner voice the conscience also points to God's presence, guiding us in truth and reminding us of His ways. But as you reflect on prophecy, consider this:

If God has fulfilled every promise He has made, if history bears witness to His faithfulness, and if lives continue to be transformed by His Word, isn't it time to believe?

I believe. Why don't you?

Chapter 7: The Voice Within

Conscience and the Inner Witness of the Holy Spirit

Many today treat the idea of conscience or inner guidance as emotional instinct or psychological conditioning. But Scripture teaches that there is something much deeper at work in the human soul a divine voice that speaks, corrects, comforts, and leads. That voice is not fantasy. It is not folklore. It is the Spirit of the Living God, bearing witness to the truth.

When skeptics call the Bible a fairytale, they ignore the evidence of God's voice that speaks through its pages and through the hearts of those who believe. They dismiss the power of the Spirit who convicts and transforms lives. But for those who have walked with God, the voice within is not imagination. It is reality.

Conscience: God's Built-In Alarm

The conscience is not just a cultural product. Romans 2:14–15 declares that even those without the Law "do by nature things required by the law," because the law is "written on their hearts." That internal voice that sense of right and wrong is evidence that a moral God created us.

When a person feels guilt after lying or regret after hurting someone, it is not evolution or ethics it is God's Spirit awakening the conscience. The voice within us calls us back to truth, justice, and grace. That voice is not from a storybook; it is from the Creator Himself.

A Still, Small Voice Not Thunder, But Truth

The prophet Elijah experienced something many of us miss. In 1 Kings 19, God showed him that His presence was not in the wind, earthquake, or fire. It was in a still, small voice a whisper that moved Elijah to listen, reflect, and obey.

That same Spirit whispers to us today. The Bible is not a dead book. It breathes. Hebrews 4:12 tells us that the Word of God is "alive and active," and it "judges the thoughts and attitudes of the heart." How can something fictional search our hearts? How can myth convict sin? It cannot.

But the living Word can. And the Spirit of God uses that Word to speak within us.

Not a Fairytale a Transforming Power

The voice within has real-world impact. Ask any believer who has resisted temptation, chosen forgiveness, or changed direction in life because of a quiet nudge from God. These are not coincidences. They are confirmations.

In John 16:13, Jesus said the Holy Spirit would "guide you into all truth." Not half-truth. Not moral symbolism. Truth. This promise proves that God wants a real relationship with us one where He still speaks.

And when He does, it is not fantasy. It is fruit. The fruits of the Spirit love, joy, peace, patience, kindness are not abstract ideas. They are lived-out realities in the lives of people who hear and obey the voice of God.

Why the World Denies It

People scoff at the idea of God's inner voice because they want a god they can control. A god who never convicts them. A god who never tells them "No." But the real God speaks. And when He does, His voice cuts through the noise, calling us to holiness, humility, and truth.

John 10:27 records Jesus saying, "My sheep listen to my voice; I know them, and they follow me." The world does not hear His voice because they do not belong to Him. But believers hear it not audibly, but undeniably.

That is not imagination. That is relationship.

The Conscience of a Child

Even children, before they are taught theology or doctrine, feel that voice within. A child who sneaks a cookie and hides it is not acting out of fear of rules they are responding to something deeper. That is not superstition. That is the Spirit of God planting seeds of righteousness in young hearts.

Jesus said in Matthew 18:3, "Unless you become like little children, you will never enter the kingdom of heaven." Why? Because children believe in what they feel before the world teaches them to doubt. They are still soft to the Spirit's whisper. Sadly, many adults grow deaf to it.

Biblical Examples of Conscience and the Spirit's Voice

The Bible is filled with people who heard and responded to the voice within sometimes obeying and sometimes resisting. Their stories reveal just how real and active the Holy Spirit is in guiding those who belong to God.

Take Peter, for example. After denying Jesus three times, he heard the rooster crow and was at once struck with guilt. The Bible says in Luke 22:62 that Peter "went outside and wept bitterly." What caused that sorrow? It was not fear of punishment it was conviction. The voice within had spoken, and Peter's heart responded. Later, restored by Jesus, Peter became a powerful voice of truth, leading the early church. His transformation was not the result of a moral fairytale; it was the outcome of a living encounter.

Consider the apostle Paul. Before his conversion, he was known as Saul a man who persecuted Christians with zeal. But when he met Jesus on the road to Damascus, everything changed. In Acts 9, we see a proud man struck blind and humbled. God sent Ananias to heal him and confirm his calling. Saul became Paul, not because he read an inspiring myth, but because he experienced the living Christ and the Spirit took hold of his life.

And what about David? The man after God's own heart made tragic mistakes adultery, deceit, even murder. Yet when confronted by the prophet Nathan, David did not make excuses. He responded with repentance. Psalm 51 is a raw and honest cry: "Create in me a pure heart, O God, and renew a steadfast spirit within me." David knew the difference between guilt and godly sorrow. He did not need a bedtime story. He needed and found restoration through the Spirit of God.

A Personal Reflection

There have been moments in my life where no sermon, no friend, and no circumstance could have reached me the way the Spirit did. One evening, in the middle of a silent room, I felt the weight of a poor decision I had made. No one else knew about it. There was no outward shame. But inside, my heart was heavy.

I opened my Bible and read Psalm 32: "When I kept silent, my bones wasted away through my groaning all day long... Then I acknowledged my sin to you and did not cover up my iniquity." That verse hit me like a bolt of lightning. The Spirit was not shouting but He was speaking. I confessed, repented, and found peace. Not because of a story. Not because of some hopeful idea. Because the God of Scripture is alive and He still speaks to His children.

That moment did not change my theology. It changed my relationship with God. It deepened my trust in the Bible not as a book of religious sayings, but as a lifeline to truth, grace, and holiness.

The Spirit Still Speaks

We live in a noisy world, full of distractions, confusion, and cynicism. But God is not silent. He is still speaking through His Word, through His Spirit, and through that gentle nudge in your soul. The voice within is real. And it is rooted in Scripture.

Do not let anyone convince you that the Bible is a collection of tales or moral lessons. It is the living Word of a living God. And the Holy

Spirit, who inspired every word, now lives in us reminding, correcting, comforting, and guiding.

If you feel a stirring in your heart as you read these words, that is not emotion. That is invitation. The Spirit may be speaking to you now. The question is will you listen?

A Closing Prayer

Heavenly Father,

Thank You for giving us not only Your written Word, but also Your living presence through the Holy Spirit.

Thank You for the voice within that quiet, convicting, comforting guide who draws us back to truth when we drift.

Help us to listen more carefully, obey more quickly, and trust more fully.

Let our consciences be shaped by Your Word, not the world.

And may we never forget that You are not a distant story we serve a risen Savior who still speaks.

We believe, Lord. Help those who doubt. Speak louder than the noise of culture.

Whisper through the chaos.

Let Your still, small voice guide us all our days.

In Jesus' name, Amen.

Chapter 8: The Person of Jesus Christ

If you are searching for proof that God is real, look no further than Jesus Christ. His life, teachings, miracles, death, and resurrection provide the clearest, most compelling evidence of God's existence and love. For those who met Him, He was not just a wise teacher or a moral guide He was the Son of God, the living proof of divine power.

I believe because I have met the truth of Jesus. Why don't you?

A Historical Foundation

Unlike myths or legends, the life of Jesus is firmly rooted in history. Ancient sources both Christian and non-Christian attest to His existence. Roman historians like Tacitus and Suetonius, the Jewish historian Josephus, and early Christian writings all confirm that Jesus lived, taught, was crucified under Pontius Pilate, and that His followers claimed He rose from the dead.

The Gospels Mathew, Mark, Luke, and John are eyewitness accounts, written within the lifetimes of those who knew Jesus. They describe not only His teachings but also His miracles: calming storms, healing the sick, raising the dead, feeding thousands, and casting out demons. These were not just moral lessons they were demonstrations of divine authority.

His Claims Set Him Apart

What makes Jesus unique is not just what He did but what He claimed. He did not merely point to God; He claimed to be God. In John 10:30, Jesus said, "I and the Father are one." In John 14:6, He declared, "I am the way, the truth, and the life. No one comes to the Father except through me."

No other religious leader Buddha, Muhammad, Confucius claimed to be God incarnate. Jesus' bold declarations force us to make a choice: was He a liar, a lunatic, or the Lord? As C.S. Lewis wrote in Mere Christianity:

"A man who was merely a man and said the sort of things Jesus said would not be a great moral teacher. He would either be a lunatic or else he would be the Devil of Hell. You must make your choice."

The Cross and the Empty Tomb

Jesus' crucifixion was a historical event witnessed by many. But the resurrection is what sets Him apart. The tomb was empty. The guards fled. Over 500 people claimed to have seen Him alive after His death (1 Corinthians 15:6). The disciples, once terrified, boldly preached His resurrection, many dying as martyrs rather than deny the truth.

If the resurrection were a hoax, how do we explain the courage of these early believers? Liars do not die for their lies. Something transformative happened something powerful enough to ignite a global movement that continues to this day.

A Personal Encounter

I can share stories of prophecy, moral conviction, or creation's complexity, but nothing compares to knowing Jesus personally. His presence in my life is undeniable. His peace has steadied me in storms; His love has healed my broken places; His truth has given me purpose.

There was a time, after moving to Florida and facing uncertainty, when I doubted everything. I questioned whether I had made the right decisions. I wrestled with fear and frustration. In those moments, I turned to Jesus not just in prayer, but in desperate surrender. I opened my Bible and read His words in Matthew 11:28-30:

"Come to me, all you who are weary and burdened, and I will give you rest. Take my yoke upon you and learn from me, for I am gentle and humble in heart, and you will find rest for your souls. For my yoke is easy and my burden is light."

I felt His presence wash over me, calming my anxious heart. It was not just words it was Him, alive and present, offering peace. That encounter changed me. It deepened my faith, anchored me in His love, and reminded me that God is not distant or theoretical. He is nearby. He is real.

A Testimony of Transformation

Let me tell you about my friend, Joe (name changed). Joe was an alcoholic for over twenty years. He had lost his job, his family, and his dignity. One night, at his lowest point, he found himself sitting in a cold church pew at a recovery meeting. The speaker shared about Jesus about forgiveness, grace, and the power to change. Something inside Joe broke. He went home, knelt by his bed, and cried out, "Jesus, if you're real, please help me!"

Joe's life changed overnight. He poured out every bottle he owned, called his estranged wife and apologized, and started attending church regularly. It was not easy rebuilding trust, facing the consequences of his past but Joe was different. He was sober, hopeful, and filled with a peace he had never known. Today, he leads recovery groups and shares his story, always pointing back to Jesus.

The Universal Invitation

Jesus did not come just for a select few. His invitation is for everyone no matter your past, your doubts, your struggles. He said in John 3:16:

"For God so loved the world that he gave his one and only Son, that whoever believes in him shall not perish but have eternal life."

His arms are open wide. He offers forgiveness, new life, and hope not because we deserve it, but because He loves us.

Why Don't You Believe?

If you are searching for evidence of God, look to Jesus. Read His words. Reflect on His life. Consider the empty tomb. Listen to the testimonies of those whose lives He has transformed.

I believe because I know Him not just as a historical figure, but as my Savior, my Friend, my Lord. Why don't you?

A Closing Reflection

As we prepare for the next chapter, where we will explore how Jesus' presence leads us into a deeper relationship with God, take a moment to consider:

- Have you encountered Jesus personally?
- Have you allowed His love to penetrate your heart?
- Are you ready to take a step of faith and say, "Jesus, I believe"?

I believe. Why don't you?

Chapter 9: Deepening the Relationship with God

Belief is not the end of faith it is the beginning. What God truly desires is a relationship with us. Not something distant or religiously robotic, but something real, personal, and alive.

You may believe there is a God. That is good. But God wants more than belief He wants connection. He does not want you just sitting in a pew once a week; He wants to walk with you through your daily life. Through tears and triumphs, through prayers and problems, through mornings when you feel strong and nights when you cannot take another step.

"Come near to God and He will come near to you."

James 4:8 (NIV)

From Belief to Bond

We often settle for acknowledging God but never invite Him deeper. That would be like being married and only talking to your spouse on holidays. That is not a relationship it is distance.

But when you lean into God when you seek Him, talk with Him, cry to Him, ask Him, thank Him your faith begins to shift from belief to bond. He becomes not just your Creator, but your Companion.

"Draw near to God, and he will draw near to you."

James 4:8 (ESV)

"The Lord is close to the brokenhearted and saves those who are crushed in spirit."

Psalm 34:18 (NIV)

My Testimony: $400 and a Knock on the Door

Let me tell you about the day my faith deepened forever.

In 2007, my wife had a massive stroke. She had been the primary source of income for our household, bringing in two-thirds of what we needed to survive. After the stroke, she could no longer work.

Our finances crumbled overnight.

We were trying to get by, but it felt like every month, another crisis came knocking. And then came December. A $400 car insurance payment was due. I did not have the money. I did not know how I was going to make it work.

Still, I did not want to avoid the situation. I told my insurance agent I would stop by and talk with him.

I will never forget that drive.

I was praying through tears pleading with God for help, guidance, intervention anything. It was not a rehearsed prayer. It was raw, broken, desperate.

"Lord, I need You. I cannot do this. I need You to move."

What happened next still shakes me to my core.

Years earlier, I had done computer work for my insurance agent. When I walked into his office that day, he did not mention the $400 payment. Instead, he said:

"Go next door. The pawn shop owner needs your help."

I was confused, but I obeyed.

The pawn shop owner explained that he needed four computers networked and someone to train his staff on their pawn software. He asked if I could do it. I said yes.

He asked the price, my reply $1,600 for the job. Then he handed me a check right there on the spot a $400 deposit.

The exact amount I needed.

That was not luck. That was not coincidence. That was God showing up at the exact moment I needed Him most.

"Before they call, I will answer; while they are still speaking, I will hear."

Isaiah 65:24 (NIV)

Prayer Works Even When the Answer Is not Immediate

Many people lose faith because they think God did not answer their prayer. But here is the truth:

God always answers.

Sometimes He says yes.

Sometimes He says no.

Sometimes He says wait.

And sometimes... He says, "I've got something better."

But He always answers because He always hears.

"This is the confidence we have in approaching God: that if we ask anything according to His will, He hears us."

1 John 5:14 (NIV)

"Ask and it will be given to you; seek and you will find; knock and the door will be opened to you."

Matthew 7:7 (NIV)

"You do not have because you do not ask God."

James 4:2 (NIV)

These verses are not spiritual guarantees of instant gratification. They are invitations to relationship. When we seek God, we draw close to His heart and that changes the way we pray.

Sometimes, what we want is not what we need. And sometimes, what we pray for is not ready to be delivered yet. But trust this: God hears you. God sees you. And God answers in the way that is best for you.

God Is not a Vending Machine He is a Father

Too often, we treat God like a cosmic vending machine. Press the right buttons, say the right words, and get what we want.

But God is not a vending machine He is a Father.

A good father does not give his child a box of matches just because they ask for it. He gives what is good what will help, not harm.

> "Which of you, if your son asks for bread, will give him a stone? Or if he asks for a fish, will give him a snake? If you then... know how to give good gifts... how much more will your Father in heaven give good gifts to those who ask Him!"

Matthew 7:9–11 (NIV)

Faith Deepens in the Waiting

I will be honest. That $400 story was not the only time I have prayed in desperation. There were other times the answers did not come so quickly.

I have prayed for healing and had to wait.

I have prayed for peace and still battled anxiety.

I have prayed for provision and had to walk a tightrope of faith.

But even in the waiting, even in the silence, God was there. He used those seasons to grow my character, to stretch my trust, to prepare me for the next step.

> "Let us then approach God's throne of grace with confidence, so that we may receive mercy and find grace to help us in our time of need."

Hebrews 4:16 (NIV)

Real Faith Is Not Just in Big Miracles

That moment with the $400 check was not flashy. There were no angels, no thunder, no voice from heaven. But it was just as miraculous because it was perfectly timed.

It was quiet, but it was clear. And it was God.

You do not need giant miracles to believe. You need real moments like that when you see God working in your life in undeniable ways.

He may work through people, conversations, job opportunities, even strangers. But when you have eyes to see Him, you will find His fingerprints everywhere.

> "In all your ways acknowledge Him, and He will make your paths straight."

Proverbs 3:6 (ESV)

Keep Asking. Keep Seeking. Keep Knocking.

If you are in a season where it feels like God is quiet do not give up. talking to Him. Keep asking. Keep looking for. Keep knocking.

Sometimes the very act of prayer is what changes us.

> "Then Jesus told his disciples... that they should always pray and not give up."

Luke 18:1 (NIV)

> "The prayer of a righteous person is powerful and effective."

James 5:16 (NIV)

> "Evening, morning and noon I cry out... and He hears my voice."

Psalm 55:17 (NIV)

God is not slow to answer. He is perfect in timing.

Closing Thoughts: A Relationship Worth Everything

I have lived through storms I never saw coming. I have had days when I was on my knees, begging God for a breakthrough. But I can look back now and say with full confidence:

God was always there.

When my wife had her stroke, God carried us.

When I did not have the $400, He made a way.

When I had no words left to pray, He still listened.

That is not religion. That is relationship.

> "Here I am! I stand at the door and knock. If anyone hears My voice and opens the door, I will come in..."

Revelation 3:20 (NIV)

So, I Ask You...

Do you believe in God?

Or do you know Him?

Do you trust Him with your needs?

Do you talk to Him daily?

He is already knocking.

He is already listening.

He is already making a way.

I believe. Why don't you?

Chapter 10: If You Don't Believe Because of Lack of Evidence, This Chapter is for You

Some people say, "I want to believe, but there just isn't enough evidence." They want something concrete proof that God is real, beyond feelings or faith. If that is you, this chapter is for you. Let us walk through several pieces of physical evidence, supported by historical, archaeological, and scientific findings, that point directly to the existence of God and the truth of His Word.

I believe because the evidence speaks. Why don't you?

1. The Dead Sea Scrolls: Proof of Scripture's Preservation

In 1947, a young Bedouin shepherd stumbled upon jars containing ancient scrolls in the caves of Qumran, near the Dead Sea. These scrolls, dating back over 2,000 years, include copies of almost every book in the Hebrew Bible, along with other writings. Known as the Dead Sea Scrolls, they revolutionized biblical studies.

Before their discovery, some skeptics claimed that the Bible we read today had been corrupted over centuries of copying. But when scholars compared the Dead Sea Scrolls with modern Hebrew texts, they were astonished. The texts were nearly identical, with only minor variations none affecting core doctrines.

This physical evidence shows that Scripture has been faithfully preserved, reinforcing the reliability of God's Word. It is as if God left these scrolls in the desert for us to find at the right time a reminder that His truth endures.

2. Archaeological Evidence of Biblical Events

Many dismiss the Bible's historical accounts as myths or legends. Yet archaeology has repeatedly confirmed its details. Here are some key examples:

The Pool of Siloam: Mentioned in John 9, where Jesus healed a man born blind. For centuries, scholars thought it was fictional, but in 2004, archaeologists uncovered it stays in Jerusalem, exactly where the Bible described.

The Tel Dan Stele: This stone slab, discovered in 1993, bears an inscription referring to the "House of David," confirming King David's historical existence. Before this, some doubted David was a real person.

The Cyrus Cylinder: Found in Babylon, this artifact records King Cyrus's decree allowing Jewish exiles to return to their land, aligning perfectly with Ezra 1:1-4.

The Hittite Empire: Once thought to be a biblical invention, evidence of the Hittites was discovered in the early 20th century, confirming their prominence during biblical times.

These discoveries show that the Bible is not just a spiritual guide it is a reliable historical record, rooted in physical reality.

3. The Fine-Tuning of the Universe

Physics reveals a universe so precisely calibrated for life that it defies natural explanation. Scientists have identified over 30 fundamental physical constants like the strength of gravity, the speed of light, and the cosmological constant that are finely tuned. Even the slightest change in these values would make life impossible.

For example, if gravity were just slightly stronger, stars would burn out quickly; if slightly weaker, they would not form at all. The odds of these constants aligning perfectly by chance are astronomically small akin to tossing a dart from Earth and hitting a coin on the moon.

This fine-tuning suggests intelligent design. The universe is not a random accident; it was created with purpose, echoing Psalm 19:1: "The heavens declare the glory of God; the skies proclaim the work of his hands."

4. The Complexity of Life: DNA and the Cell

Inside every living cell is DNA, a molecule containing the instructions for building and maintaining life. This "genetic code" is written in a four-letter alphabet (A, T, C, G), forming sequences that tell cells what proteins to produce. The information in just one cell's DNA could fill thousands of books.

Scientists agree that DNA operates like a language complex, ordered, and purposeful. But where did this language come from? Natural processes alone cannot account for the origin of such intricate information. It points to a Mind behind life, a Creator who designed the code.

As Francis Collins, a geneticist and leader of the Human Genome Project, wrote:

"The God of the Bible is also the God of the genome. He can be worshiped in the cathedral or in the laboratory."

5. Jesus' Resurrection: Historical and Physical Evidence

The resurrection of Jesus is not just a spiritual claim it is a historical event with physical evidence. The empty tomb, the eyewitness accounts, and the dramatic transformation of the disciples all point to a real, physical resurrection.

Here are key facts:

The tomb was found empty by women, whose testimony was less valued in that culture if the story were fabricated, this detail would not be included.

Roman guards and a sealed tomb make theft unlikely.

Over 500 witnesses (1 Corinthians 15:6) reported seeing the risen Jesus.

The disciples, once fearful, boldly proclaimed the resurrection, many dying as martyrs.

If Jesus did not rise, why would so many willingly face death for a lie? The resurrection is the ultimate physical evidence of God's power and the truth of the Gospel.

6. Evidence from Prophecy Fulfillment

The Bible contains hundreds of prophecies specific predictions about events, nations, and people, many fulfilled with astonishing accuracy. For instance:

Isaiah 53 describes the suffering servant, pierced for our sins, fulfilled in Jesus' crucifixion.

Psalm 22 details a crucifixion scene, written centuries before crucifixion was even used.

Ezekiel 26 foretells Tyre's destruction, fulfilled when Alexander the Great's forces used its ruins to build a causeway.

These fulfilled prophecies are physical, verifiable evidence that God knows and directs history.

7. Natural Revelation: Creation Itself

Scripture tells us in Romans 1:20:

"For since the creation of the world God's invisible qualities his eternal power and divine nature have been clearly seen, being understood from what has been made, so that people are without excuse."

Creation itself mountains, oceans, stars, the intricate balance of ecosystems bears witness to a Creator. Scientists studying irreducible complexity, like the bacterial flagellum (a microscopic motor), admit that natural processes cannot explain these structures. The design is too precise, too purposeful.

A Personal Reflection

I have met God's reality not just in scripture but in the world around me. When I stood by the ocean at sunrise, watching the sky transform with color, I felt His presence. When I held my grandchild for the first time, marveling at the delicate fingers and soft breaths, I knew this was no accident of biology.

I believe because the evidence both seen and unseen testifies to a loving, powerful Creator. Why don't you?

A Challenge and an Invitation

If you have been waiting for evidence, consider this:

- The Bible's preservation through centuries and archaeological validation.
- The fine-tuning of the universe and the intricate design of life.
- The undeniable impact of Jesus' life, death, and resurrection.
- The fulfillment of prophecies, witnessed by history.

All this points to one truth: God is real, and He is inviting you to know Him.

A Closing Prayer

Heavenly Father,

Thank You for the evidence You have provided through history, science, nature, and the life of Jesus. Open my eyes to see Your hand in the world around me and in my own life. When I doubt, remind me of Your faithfulness. When I question, speak truth to my heart. Lead me to a deeper understanding of Your love and a stronger faith in Your reality. I believe, Lord. Help my unbelief. In Jesus' name, Amen.

Chapter 11: Conclusion From Doubt to Faith

If you have journeyed through this book, you have seen how the evidence through history, science, archaeology, and personal stories points unmistakably to the existence of God. We have walked through fulfilled prophecies, the fine-tuning of the universe, the undeniable transformation of lives, and the compelling life and resurrection of Jesus Christ.

Yet, despite the evidence, doubt may still linger. That is natural. Faith is not the absence of doubt; it is the decision to trust in spite of it.

I believe because I have wrestled with doubt and found faith stronger. Why don't you?

The Reality of Doubt

You may be thinking: "I am not ready to believe. I still have questions. I need more time, more proof." That is okay. God is not afraid of your doubts. In fact, He invites them. In Mark 9:24, a desperate father cried out to Jesus, "I believe; help my unbelief!" Jesus did not scold him. Instead, He responded with compassion, healing the man's son.

Doubt can be a steppingstone, not an obstacle. It can lead us to deeper understanding and stronger faith. The key is not to let doubt keep you stuck, but to let it drive you to seek the truth.

Faith Is a Journey

Faith is not a destination we arrive at overnight. It is a journey a path we walk, step by step, trusting that God will guide us. Along the way, we may stumble, question, and wrestle. But as we continue seeking, God meets us with His grace.

The Bible reminds us in Hebrews 11:1:

"Now faith is confidence in what we hope for and assurance about what we do not see."

Faith does not erase every doubt or answer every question. It is the choice to believe based on the evidence we have seen and the peace we have felt in our hearts.

A Personal Reflection

I have faced moments of deep doubt in my lifetimes when the weight of circumstances made me question everything. When I lost loved ones, when I faced career setbacks, when I felt overwhelmed by uncertainty, I wondered if God was truly there.

But in those dark times, I discovered something powerful: God is not threatened by our questions. In fact, it is often in our moments of greatest doubt that He reveals Himself most clearly. Through prayer, Scripture, and the support of faithful friends, I found reassurance. God was still their patient, loving, and faithful.

An Invitation to Take the Next Step

If you have reached the end of this book and you are still unsure about faith, let me encourage you: do not stop here. Keep seeking. Ask your questions. Pray, even if you are not sure anyone is listening.

Most importantly, find a local church. Church is not just a building or a weekly ritual. It is a community of people who are on the same journey people who have questions, doubts, and struggles, just like you. In a local church, you will find:

Support: People who will walk with you through life's difficulties.

Teaching: Biblical truths that strengthen your understanding of God.

Worship: A chance to connect with God through music, prayer, and reflection.

Opportunities to Serve: Ways to put your faith into action and make a difference.

When you step into a church, you are not signing away your questions or agreeing to blind faith. You are opening yourself to God's presence and giving Him a chance to meet you where you are.

Why the Church Matters

The early church was not a perfect institution it was a group of ordinary people transformed by Jesus' love. They supported each other, shared what they had, prayed together, and lived out their faith in everyday life. Acts 2:42-47 describes this beautifully:

"They devoted themselves to the apostles' teaching and to fellowship, to the breaking of bread and to prayer... All the believers were together and had everything in common... And the Lord added to their number daily those who were being saved."

Today's churches, though imperfect, are still communities where God works powerfully. Whether it's a large congregation or a small group, a traditional service or a contemporary gathering, there's a place where you can belong, ask questions, and grow.

The Crossroads

At this point, you stand at a crossroads. You can continue searching alone, trying to figure everything out on your own. Or you can take a step of faith however small and say, "God, if You're real, show me. I'm open to knowing You."

Faith isn't about having all the answers. It's about being willing to trust, to open your heart, and to take the first step.

A Testimony of a New Beginning

I once knew a man named Tom (name changed) who wrestled with doubt for decades. He had read countless books, attended debates, and asked every question imaginable. But one Sunday, out of curiosity, he visited a local church. During the service, the pastor shared a message about God's love and faithfulness. Tom felt something shift in his heart a sense of peace he couldn't explain.

He didn't suddenly become a believer that day. But he kept coming back. He joined a small group, asked his questions, and listened. Over time, as he saw the love of God in the lives of others and experienced it himself, his doubt gave way to faith. Today, Tom serves as a leader in his church, mentoring others who are where he once was.

I Believe. Why Don't You?

Throughout this book, I've shared evidence, stories, and truths that have strengthened my faith. But faith is a personal decision.

I believe because I've seen God's hand in my life, in the world around me, and in the lives of countless others. I believe because His Word stands firm, His promises are true, and His love is unchanging.

Why don't you?

A Closing Prayer

Heavenly Father,

Thank You for walking with me through doubt and uncertainty. Thank You for showing me that faith isn't about having all the answers, but about trusting in You. Lord, I open my heart to You today. Help me move from doubt to faith, from questions to confidence. Surround me with people who will encourage and support my journey. Lead me to a local church where I can learn, grow, and serve. I believe, Lord. Help my unbelief. In Jesus' name, Amen.

Your Next Step

As you close this book, don't close the door on faith. Find a Bible-believing local church. Connect with others who can walk alongside you. Continue reading Scripture. Pray, even if your words feel small.

Faith is a journey. Take the first step today.

Reflection Questions – Page 1

1. What does the phrase "The Bible is not a fairytale" mean to you personally?
2. Have you ever doubted your faith? What caused it, and what helped you through it?
3. How would you explain your belief in God to someone who has never opened a Bible?

Reflection Questions – Page 2

1. What are some common reasons people stop believing in church or Scripture today?
2. How can the Church better reach people who think God is silent or distant?
3. In what ways can your personal story be used to inspire someone struggling with doubt?

Reflection Questions – Page 3

1. Do you believe that God still speaks to people today? Why or why not?
2. How do you distinguish between your own thoughts and the "still small voice" of the Holy Spirit?
3. What Scriptures do you turn to when your faith is shaken?

Reflection Questions – Page 4

1. Have you ever witnessed a moment where God clearly intervened in someone's life? Describe it.
2. Why is it important to share your faith story, even if it feels imperfect or unfinished?
3. What would you say to someone who asks, "If God is real, why doesn't He stop suffering?"

Reflection Questions – Page 5

1. What are some practical steps you can take to grow stronger in your faith this year?
2. How can churches restore trust with people who feel burned or abandoned by religion?
3. If Jesus sat down next to you right now, what would you want to ask Him?

A Closing Word from the Author

To every person who held this book in their hands, who turned its pages, whether out of curiosity, hope, skepticism, or faith I want to thank you. I do not take lightly the time you have given to read these words, wrestle with the questions they raise, and explore the belief that burns deeply within me.

This was never just a book to me. It was a calling. A fire in my bones I could not ignore. I wrote this not because I claim to have all the answers, but because I have wrestled with many of the same questions you have. I have stared into the storm of doubt. I have sat in silence, wondering if God was listening. I have known the heartbreak of unanswered prayers, the sting of judgment, and the weight of wondering whether faith was still worth holding onto.

Yet through it all, something greater than me has always called me back. That voice not loud, but steady whispering, "Keep believing." That presence not always seen, but always near guiding me back to Jesus Christ.

If you have read this book and come to the end, my prayer is simple and sincere: that you are closer to God than when you first began. You came already walking with Him, seeking encouragement to keep going. You came doubting, wondering if the Bible could really be more than an ancient tale. Or, just maybe, you picked up this book not even knowing what you were searching for, but God knew.

Whatever your starting point, I thank you for trusting me to walk part of this journey with you. My hope is not that you remember my name, or even this title, but that something within these pages stirred your soul. That something whispered to your heart, "There is more. There is truth. There is grace. There is Jesus."

I want you to know that you are not alone in your questions. You are not strange for your doubts. Even the greatest heroes of the Bible cried out to God in moments of weakness and uncertainty. David asked,

"Why, Lord, do you stand far off?" (Psalm 10:1). Job questioned why the righteous suffer. Thomas needed to see the scars before he could believe. And yet, through all their questions, God remained faithful.

Faith is not the absence of doubt. It is the decision to trust even when the outcome is unclear. It is holding on to God even when you are not sure He is holding on to you. And let me assure you He is.

If this book helped rekindle your belief, I give God all the glory. If it gave you a reason to open the Bible again, to whisper a prayer you had not spoken in years, or to sit quietly and say, "Lord, if You're real, show me," then it was worth every hour spent writing.

Some of you may have been deeply hurt by religion. You may carry scars inflicted not by God, but by people who claimed to speak in His name. I want to say: I am sorry. Those wounds are real, and they matter. But I also want to remind you: Jesus is not the one who hurt you. In fact, He is the one who longs to heal you. He came not for the perfect, but for the broken. Not to judge, but to redeem.

Others of you may be new to all this new to faith, new to Jesus, even new to hope. If something in your heart is stirring, do not silence it. That is the Holy Spirit. You do not need fancy words or church credentials to begin. All it takes is a sincere heart and a whisper: "Jesus, I believe. Help me follow You."

If you are still unsure, still questioning keep reading, keep asking, keep looking for. God is not threatened by your doubts. He is not surprised by your questions. He welcomes them. He welcomes you.

For those of you who already walk with Christ, I thank you for reading as well. My prayer for you is that this book strengthens your resolve, encourages your witness, and reminds you that your faith is not in vain. The world may be loud, but God is not silent. The Bible is not a fairytale it is the living Word of God, sharper than any two-edged sword, still speaking, still transforming, still alive.

To every pastor, teacher, small group leader, or friend who shared this book with someone else thank you. You are a bridge between the hurting and the healing, between seekers and the Savior. May you never grow tired of pointing people to the Light.

And to those who quietly read and never told a soul know that you are seen. God knows your heart. Whether you read this in a quiet bedroom, a hospital room, a jail cell, or a coffee shop, the same God who inspired these words is present with you even now.

As I close, let me offer this final prayer not just for the pages behind you, but for the life ahead of you:

Father, for every person who reads these words, I pray You draw them near. For the doubter, give light. For the seeker, give clarity. For the broken, bring healing. For the believer, bring boldness. For the lost, let them be found. Let every heart know that You are real, that You are good, and that You never stop pursuing us. In Jesus' name. Amen.

Thank you, friend, for walking this far with me.

Now, walk on with Him.

Edward Fair

Author of I Believe: Why Don't You?

Scripture References for Study and Reflection

Hebrews 11:1

Now faith is the substance of things hoped for, the evidence of things not seen.

2 Timothy 3:16–17

All Scripture is God-breathed and is useful for teaching, rebuking, correcting and training in righteousness, so that the servant of God may be thoroughly equipped for every good work.

John 20:29

Then Jesus told him, "Because you have seen me, you have believed; blessed are those who have not seen and yet have believed."

Romans 10:17

So then faith comes by hearing, and hearing by the word of God.

James 1:6

But when you ask, you must believe and not doubt, because the one who doubts is like a wave of the sea, blown and tossed by the wind.

Mark 9:24

Immediately the boy's father exclaimed, "I do believe; help me overcome my unbelief!"

Jeremiah 29:13

You will seek me and find me when you seek me with all your heart.

Psalm 119:105

Your word is a lamp to my feet and a light to my path.

John 14:6Jesus answered, "I am the way and the truth and the life. No one comes to the Father except through me."

Matthew 7:7

> Ask, and it will be given to you; seek, and you will find; knock, and the door will be opened to you.

John 3:16

> For God so loved the world that He gave His one and only Son, that whoever believes in Him shall not perish but have eternal life.

Proverbs 3:5–6

> Trust in the Lord with all your heart and lean not on your own understanding; in all your ways submit to Him, and He will make your paths straight.

Psalm 34:18

> The Lord is close to the brokenhearted and saves those who are crushed in spirit.

Romans 8:38–39

> For I am convinced that neither death nor life, neither angels nor demons... will be able to separate us from the love of God that is in Christ Jesus our Lord.

1 Peter 5:7

> Cast all your anxiety on Him because He cares for you.

Matthew 28:20b

And surely I am with you always, to the very end of the age.

Galatians 2:20

I have been crucified with Christ and I no longer live, but Christ lives in me. The life I now live in the body, I live by faith in the Son of God...

2 Corinthians 5:7

For we walk by faith, not by sight.

Isaiah 55:11

So is my word that goes out from my mouth: It will not return to me empty, but will accomplish what I desire...

www.ingramcontent.com/pod-product-compliance
Lightning Source LLC
Chambersburg PA
CBHW032216040426
42449CB00005B/625